Deep Space Discovery

SATURN
AND OTHER OUTER PLANETS

GAIL TERP

BLACK
RABBIT
BOOKS

Bolt is published by Black Rabbit Books
P.O. Box 3263, Mankato, Minnesota, 56002.
www.blackrabbitbooks.com
Copyright © 2019 Black Rabbit Books

Marysa Storm, editor; Grant Gould, designer;
Omay Ayres, photo researcher

Library of Congress Cataloging-in-Publication Data
Names: Terp, Gail, 1951- author.
Title: Saturn and other outer planets / by Gail Terp.
Description: Mankato, Minnesota : Black Rabbit Books, [2019] | Series:
Bolt. Deep space discovery | Audience: Ages 9-12. | Audience: Grades 4
to 6. | Includes bibliographical references and index.
Identifiers: LCCN 2017021069 (print) | LCCN 2017028457 (ebook) |
ISBN 9781680725384 (ebook) | ISBN 9781680724226 (library binding) |
ISBN 9781680727166 (paperback)
Subjects: LCSH: Outer planets–Juvenile literature. | Solar system–Juvenile
literature.
Classification: LCC QB659 (ebook) | LCC QB659 .T47 2019 (print) |
DDC 523.4–dc23
LC record available at https://lccn.loc.gov/2017021069

Printed in China. 3/18

Image Credits

Alamy: Science Photo Library,
24; http://voyager.jpl.nasa.gov/: NASA,
Cover (Voyager); Science Source: Corey Ford,
26 (left); Detlev van Ravenswaay, 28–29; Mark
Garlick, 9 (top); Shutterstock: Aphelleon, Cover
(Saturn); Azuzl, 22–23 (large planets, sun); Bobnevv,
23 (bttm r planets); Dotted Yeti, 1, 3; Filipe Frazao, 16
(earth); Harvepino, 16–17 (bkgd); hideto999, 12, 32;
Johan Swanepoel, 16 (core); keplar, 27 (bttm); Marc Ward,
17; molaruso, Cover; Mopic, 10–11; muratart, 26–27;
NASA images, 15; Paul Stringer, 20–21; Vadim Sadovski,
4–5, 6–7, 9 (bttm), 18, 26 (right); Yuriy Mazur, 23 (bttm
r); solarsystem.nasa.gov: NASA, 27 (top); voyager.jpl.
nasa.gov/: NASA, 31
Every effort has been made to contact copyright
holders for material reproduced in this book.
Any omissions will be rectified in subse-
quent printings if notice is given
to the publisher.

CONTENTS

CHAPTER 1
Spectacular Space......4

CHAPTER 2
The Outer Planets......13

CHAPTER 3
Outer Planet
Exploration...........25

Other Resources...........30

Spectacular

The spacecraft *Cassini* circles Saturn.

It sends amazing pictures back to Earth.

Swirling gases cover Saturn's surface.

Its huge rings spread out wide.

The Planets

People have studied Saturn and other planets since **ancient** times. They could tell the planets weren't stars. They moved across the sky differently than stars.

Planets are huge bodies that **orbit** stars. Saturn and seven other planets orbit the sun. The sun's **gravity** holds them in their paths. They make up the solar system.

Some of Saturn's rings extend 175,000 miles (281,635 kilometers) from the planet.

Gas Giants

The four planets closest to the sun are the inner planets. Earth is one of them. The four planets farthest from the sun are the outer planets. They're made mostly of gas. These planets are big. People call them the gas giants. They are Jupiter, Saturn, Uranus, and Neptune.

From 1930 to 2006, there were nine planets. In 2006, scientists relabeled the ninth planet, Pluto, a dwarf planet.

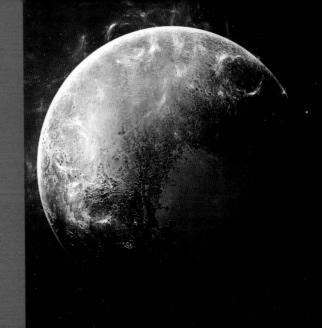

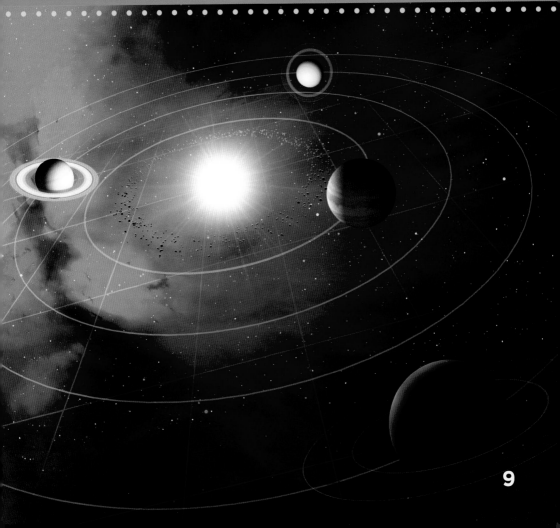

Neptune

Uranus

Saturn

Jupiter

outer planets

inner planets

Mars

Earth

Venus

Mercury

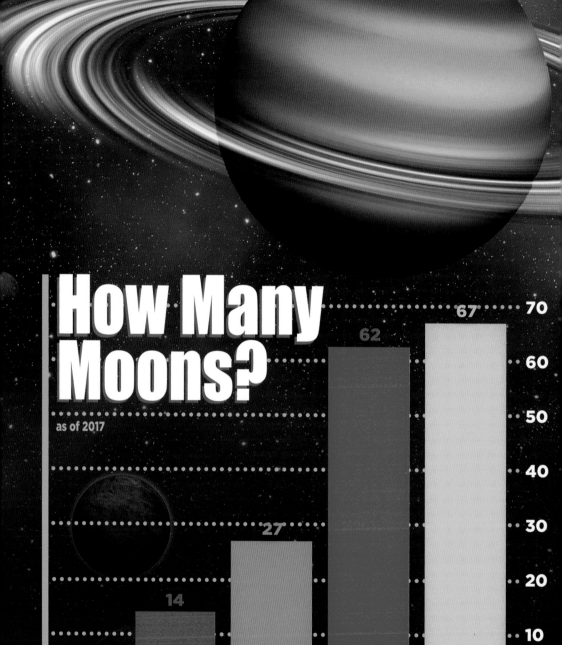

How Many Moons?

as of 2017

Planet	Moons
Neptune	14
Uranus	27
Saturn	62
Jupiter	67

CHAPTER 2

The Outer PLANETS

Saturn is known for its large rings. An **astronomer** discovered them in 1610. The rings are made from chunks of ice and rock. Some pieces of ice and rock are as small as dust. Others are as large as mountains. Saturn's rings orbit around the planet. Saturn's gravity keeps the rings in place by pulling on them.

Jupiter

Jupiter is the largest planet. Like Saturn, it has rings. The rings are hard to see, though. Jupiter's **atmosphere** is made up of swirls of gas. The gas swirls are caused by clouds and winds.

A large storm rages on Jupiter. From space, it looks big and red. People call the storm the Great Red Spot. This storm is bigger than Earth. It's gone on for more than 300 years.

Jupiter may have diamonds floating in its atmosphere. Saturn may have them too.

WHAT'S NEEDED FOR LIFE

Earth is the only planet known to have life. Scientists look for life on other planets. They believe a planet must have certain traits to support life.

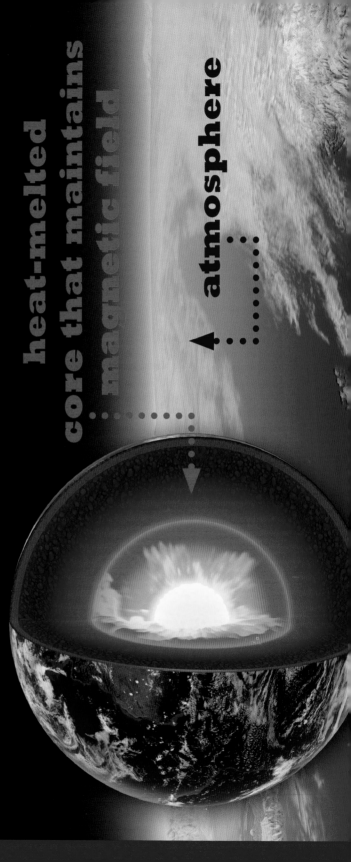

perfect distance from a star

heat-melted core that maintains magnetic field

atmosphere

liquid water

surface made
of rock

protective
magnetic
field

AVERAGE TEMPERATURES

Neptune

Uranus

Saturn

Jupiter

degrees Fahrenheit

Uranus

Uranus is the seventh planet from the sun. **Methane** gas in its atmosphere gives it a blue color. Uranus tilts more than other planets. It looks like it spins on its side. A planet's tilt gives it seasons. Because of Uranus' odd tilt, it has extreme seasons. For 21 years, sunlight only hits one side of the planet. The other side experiences a cold, dark winter.

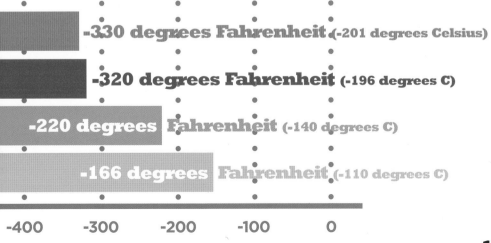

-330 degrees Fahrenheit (-201 degrees Celsius)

-320 degrees Fahrenheit (-196 degrees C)

-220 degrees Fahrenheit (-140 degrees C)

-166 degrees Fahrenheit (-110 degrees C)

-400   -300   -200   -100   0

Neptune

Neptune is the farthest planet from the sun. It has six faint rings. Like Uranus, it's blue. Neptune is quite windy. Its winds can reach more than 1,200 miles (1,931 km) per hour.

A planet's day is how long it takes to spin around once. Some planets spin faster than others. They have shorter days.

Diameter

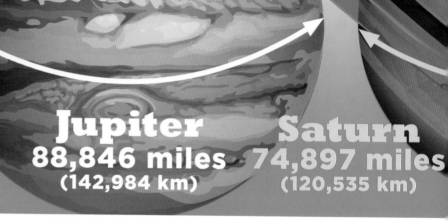

Jupiter
88,846 miles
(142,984 km)

Saturn
74,897 miles
(120,535 km)

Time to Orbit the Sun

Neptune	165 Earth years
Uranus	84 Earth years
Saturn	29 Earth years
Jupiter	12 Earth years

LENGTH OF DAY

Uranus	about **17** Earth hours
Neptune	about **16** Earth hours
Saturn	about **11** Earth hours
Jupiter	about **10** Earth hours

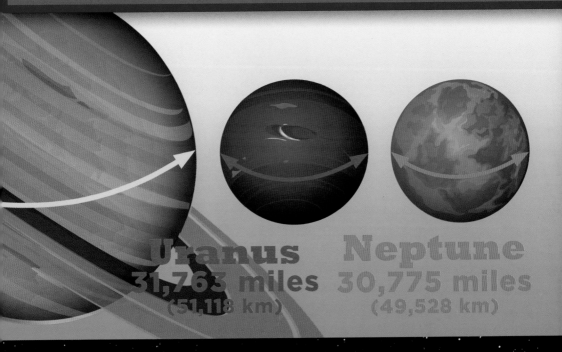

Uranus
31,763 miles
(51,118 km)

Neptune
30,775 miles
(49,528 km)

AVERAGE DISTANCE FROM THE SUN

Neptune
2.8 billion miles
(4.5 billion km)

Uranus
1.8 billion miles
(2.9 billion km)

Jupiter
484 million miles
(779 million km)

Saturn
890 million miles
(1.4 billion km)

CHAPTER 3

Outer Planet

EXPLORATION

Spacecraft from Earth first reached the gas giants in the 1970s. One flew by Jupiter in 1973. Another reached Saturn in 1979. These missions made new discoveries about each planet.

In the 1980s, *Voyager 2* traveled past the last two planets. The **probe** flew by Uranus in 1986. It reached Neptune in 1989.

21st CENTURY EXPLORATIONS AND DISCOVERIES

There have been many missions to the gas giants since 2000. Many important discoveries have been made.

2000
The spacecraft *Cassini* passes Jupiter. It takes photos.

2005
A spacecraft lands on Titan, one of Saturn's moons. It is the first to land on another planet's moon.

1999

2003
Astronomers discover five new moons around Neptune.

2004
Cassini becomes the first spacecraft to circle Saturn.

2013

A scientist studies telescope images. He discovers a new moon near Neptune.

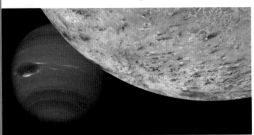

2020

2017

At the end of its mission, *Cassini* enters Saturn's atmosphere and burns up.

2016

A spacecraft travels to Jupiter. It studies the planet's atmosphere.

Future Explorations

Scientists continue to plan more missions. One spacecraft will go to Jupiter. It should reach the planet in 2030. It'll study Jupiter and its moons. There might also be a mission to Saturn. It would study Titan. A robotic submarine may even explore its sea.

Space missions bring new knowledge about the planets. The information tells people more about the solar system they call home.

Saturn

surface of Titan

ancient (AYN-shunt)—from a time long ago

astronomer (uh-STRON-uh-mer)—an expert in the science of heavenly bodies and of their sizes, motions, and composition

atmosphere (AT-muh-sfeer)—the gases that surround a planet

core (KOHR)—the central part of a planet or other body

gravity (GRAV-i-tee)—the natural force that pulls physical things toward each other

magnetic field (mag-NE-tik FEELD)—an area where an object's magnetic properties affect neighboring objects

methane (METH-eyn)—a colorless gas that has no smell and that can be burned

orbit (AWR-bit)—the path taken by one body circling around another body

probe (PRHOB)—a device used to collect information from outer space and send it back to Earth

trait (TREYT)—a characteristic or quality

BOOKS

Roumanis, Alexis. *Jupiter.* Meet the Planets. New York: Smartbook Media, Inc., 2018.

Roza, Greg. *Neptune.* Planetary Exploration. New York: Britannica Educational Publishing in association with Rosen Educational Services, 2017.

Wilkins, Mary-Jane. *The Outer Planets.* Our Solar System. Tucson, AZ: Brown Bear Books, 2017.

WEBSITES

Gas Giants: Facts about the Outer Planets
www.space.com/30372-gas-giants.html

Inner and Outer Planets
easyscienceforkids.com/inner-and-outer-planets/

Solar System Facts
www.sciencekids.co.nz/sciencefacts/space/ solarsystem.html

INDEX

C

Cassini, 4, 26–27

J

Jupiter, 8, 10, 12, 14, 15, 18–19, 22–23, 25, 26–27, 28

L

life, 16–17

M

moons, 12, 26–27, 28

N

Neptune, 8, 10, 12, 18–19, 20, 22–23, 25, 26–27

P

Pluto, 9

S

Saturn, 4, 7, 8, 10, 12, 13, 14, 15, 18–19, 22–23, 25, 26–27, 28

sizes, 14, 22–23

solar systems, 7, 10–11, 28

space exploration, 25, 26–27, 28

T

temperatures, 18–19

U

Uranus, 8, 10, 12, 18–19, 20, 22–23, 25